FIRST AMERICANS
The Comanche

SARAH De CAPUA

Marshall Cavendish
Benchmark
New York

ACKNOWLEDGMENTS

Series consultant: Raymond Bial

Marshall Cavendish Benchmark
99 White Plains Road
Tarrytown, New York 10591-9001
www.marshallcavendish.us

Text copyright © 2007 by Marshall Cavendish Corporation
Map and illustrations copyright © 2007 by Marshall Cavendish Corporation
Map and illustrations by Christopher Santoro

All Internet sites were available and accurate when sent to press.

Library of Congress Cataloging-in-Publication Data

De Capua, Sarah.
The Comanche / by Sarah De Capua.
p. cm. — (First Americans)
Includes bibliographical references and index.
ISBN-13: 978-0-7614-2249-5
ISBN-10: 0-7614-2249-8
1. Comanche Indians—History—Juvenile literature. 2. Comanche Indians—Social life and customs—Juvenile literature. I. Title.
II. Series: First Americans (Benchmark Books (Firm)
E99.C85D37 2006
978.004'974572--dc22
2006011975

Photo research by Joan Meisel
Editor: Tara T. Koellhoffer
Editorial Director: Michelle Bisson
Art Director: Anahid Hamparian
Series Designer: Symon Chow

Cover photo: Marilyn "Angel" Wynn/Nativestock.com
Alamy: 1, North Wind Picture Archives; Comanche Red River Casino: 38; Corbis: 16, Hulton-Deutsch Collection; 36, Peter Turnley;
Getty Images: 23, 34, 40, Hulton Archive; Nativestock.com: 41, Marilyn "Angel" Wynn; North Wind Picture Archives: 8, 9, 21, 32;
Raymond Bial: 4, 9, 22, 28; The Granger Collection, NY: 11, 13.

Printed in China
1 3 5 6 4 2

CONTENTS

1 · WHO ARE THE COMANCHE PEOPLE?

Members of the Comanche Nation live in Oklahoma and Texas beside their non-Indian neighbors. Their tribal headquarters is located near Lawton, Oklahoma. A large number of Comanche also lives in and around Los Angeles, California, and some Comanche live in New Mexico. In all, there are about eleven thousand Comanche living in the United States.

The Comanche call themselves Nu Mu Nu, meaning "The People." A few hundred years ago, the Comanche lived in the mountains of the present-day states of Wyoming and Montana. At that time, they were part of the Shoshone tribe. No one knows exactly why, but the Shoshone split into two groups. One group stayed in the north. The other group moved south, to what is now Colorado. This group came into contact with the Ute Indians. Many people believe it was the

The Comanche settled on the southern plains.

Ute who gave them a version of the name Comanche. Together, the Ute and Comanche traveled into what is now New Mexico in the early 1700s. There, they encountered Spanish settlers, with whom the Ute had been trading for a long time. The Ute told the Spanish that their Shoshone friends were Koh-Mahts, meaning "strangers." The Spanish began to use the word *Komantcia* to refer to the newcomers. Eventually, this word became *Comanche*.

By the mid-1700s, the Comanche became well known as the most powerful tribe of the southern plains. They lived in the area that is now southeastern Colorado, south-western Kansas, eastern New Mexico, and the central and western parts of both Oklahoma and Texas. After leaving the Shoshone, they became skilled horsemen, buffalo hunters, and warriors. They fought the Apache, Kiowa, and other Plains tribes, and took over their lands. The Comanche were so successful that they were called "Lords of the Plains." The area they controlled became known as

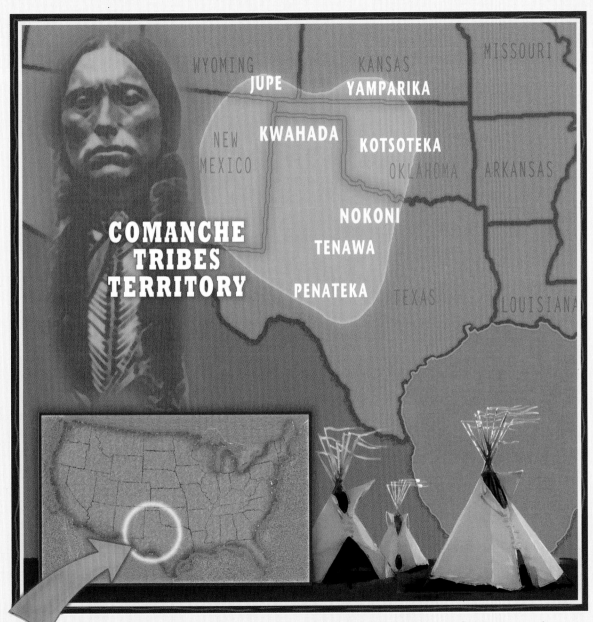

COMANCHE
TRIBES
TERRITORY

JUPE

YAMPARIKA

KWAHADA

KOTSOTEKA

NOKONI

TENAWA

PENATEKA

WYOMING

KANSAS

MISSOURI

NEW
MEXICO

OKLAHOMA

ARKANSAS

TEXAS

LOUISIANA

The Comanche lived first in the mountains of Wyoming and Montana, then moved south to their present-day territories, seen here.

the Comancheria. They dominated the sprawling Great Plains until around 1875.

A large part of the Comanche's success came when they acquired horses. Horses had been introduced to the New World in 1519, when Spanish explorers brought them to Mexico. By the end of the 1500s, the Spanish had moved

The Comanche became known as expert horse riders.

north into what is now the southwestern United States. They tried to protect their horses from the Indians, but without success. Cheyenne, Comanche, and other Plains tribes recognized how valuable horses were, and stole them from the settlers during attacks, or **raids**, on settlements. The tribes also traded for horses and captured horses that wandered

Buffalo became important to the Comanche way of life.

away from settlements. The Comanche were known for their riding skills. It was said that they were awkward and clumsy on foot but poised and graceful on horseback. The Comanche's skilled horseback riding gave them advantages in battle and buffalo hunting.

During the 1800s, important changes came to the Comanche. In 1830, the U.S. government passed the Indian Removal Act, which forced thousands of members of eastern tribes to move west to Indian Territory (present-day Oklahoma), just east of the Comancheria. The Comanche didn't like having other tribes so close, especially because members of those tribes often trespassed onto the Comancheria to hunt buffalo. There were frequent confrontations between the Comanche and the newcomers. In 1835, the U.S. government helped the Comanche make peace. An agreement was reached for the Comanche to share their hunting grounds with the eastern tribes.

In 1836, Texas won its independence from Mexico. As a result, thousands of white settlers poured into Texas. Some of the land on which they settled belonged to the Comanche. The Comanche responded by frequently raiding the new settlements. The Republic of Texas fought back by sending Texas Rangers, a specially trained force, to the Comancheria to capture the warring Comanche. This led to the Council House Massacre in 1840, in which a Comanche chief and several dozen warriors were killed. A series of attacks between settlers and Comanche followed. In 1844, a peace treaty was

In 1867, the Comanche signed a peace treaty with the U.S. government at Medicine Lodge Creek in Kansas.

Quanah Parker

Quanah Parker was born around 1850. He was the son of Peta Nocona, the chief of the Quahadi ("antelope") **band** of the Comanche, and Cynthia Ann Parker, one of the most famous white captives of any Indian tribe. Quanah Parker became chief of the Quahadi band after his father's death. At first, Parker encouraged his people to resist moving to the reservation. He led them to the Texas **Panhandle**, where they tried to hold on to their way of life. After the winter of 1874–1875, however, during which many Comanche suffered and died, Quanah Parker led his people to the reservation at Fort Sill, Oklahoma.

In the years that followed, Parker helped his people adopt a new way of life as ranchers and farmers. He became a successful rancher, business-man, and judge who decided Indian issues, and leader of all the bands of Comanche. Parker and his seven wives and twenty-five children lived in a large white house in Cache, Oklahoma. It had big white stars painted on its red roof. Some people respected Quanah Parker so much that they called his home the Comanche White House. Parker became famous throughout the United States for his wisdom and love of peace. He even had his friend, President Theodore Roosevelt, visit for dinner and wolf hunting on the reservation. Parker continued to lead his people until his death in 1911.

Quanah Parker became one of the most famous and influential leaders of the Comanche people.

signed between Texas and the Comanche, but both sides repeatedly broke it.

Texas became the twenty-eighth U.S. state in 1845. By the mid-1850s, thousands more settlers had moved into Texas. The U.S. government had set aside reservation land there and Indians in the state were expected to move to it. Most of the Comanche, however, refused to leave the Comancheria even though they were losing their land and their horse and buffalo herds were getting smaller.

In October 1867, nearly five thousand Comanche, Kiowa, Kiowa-Apache, Arapaho, and Cheyenne traveled to Medicine Lodge Creek in Kansas to meet with U.S. government officials. There, the Treaty of Medicine Lodge Creek was signed. In exchange for houses, farms, farming equipment, and tools, and cattle, the Indians gave up most of their land but kept hunting grounds in parts of the Comancheria in present-day southern Kansas and the Texas Panhandle. Many Comanche rejected the agreement and refused to leave the Comancheria. By the end of the harsh winter of 1875, however, the

Comanche knew they could not stop the whites from moving onto their lands. They saw that they were losing their way of life. For their own survival, they gave up the Comancheria and moved to the reservation. Their reign over the southern Great Plains was over.

2 · LIFE ON THE SOUTHERN PLAINS

When the Comanche moved to the Great Plains, they built tepees. These were better suited to their lifestyle of moving often to follow the buffalo herds. Tepees could be set up and taken down easily. The tepees were made of cedar or pine poles that were about 14 feet (4 m) long. To put up the tepee, women tied four of the poles together to make a frame. They set them upright and spread out the legs. Then they placed about twenty shorter poles around the frame. Buffalo hides, sometimes as many as twenty, were sewn together to cover the tepee. The doorway, covered by a buffalo hide, always faced east—toward the rising sun.

The Comanche had a loosely organized tribal structure. Each Comanche belonged to family hunting bands of various sizes. The Comanche could live in a band with relatives but

The Comanche lived in villages of many tepees.

were not required to do so. They could join other bands or start their own. Over time, several bands developed, each living and hunting on its own portion of the Comancheria. The bands included the Kotsoteka ("buffalo eaters"), the Nokoni ("people who return"), the Penateka ("honey eaters"), the Quahadi or Kwahada ("antelope"), and the Yamparika ("root eaters"). These groups shared a language and culture, but they were independent. Central to each group was the band council, which made important decisions, such as when to move and when to hunt, for everyone in the band. All the adult male members of the band belonged to the council. Each band also had a war chief and a peace chief.

Comanche families were made up of parents, children, grandparents, and aunts and uncles. Grandmothers helped with chores in and around the tepee and looked after the children. Men were the heads of the families. Bands were determined by male relatives: fathers, sons, and brothers.

The role of Comanche men was to hunt, make tools, and

protect their families. Besides buffalo, the Comanche hunted black bears, antelope, elk, and sometimes deer. They trapped wolves and foxes for their fur. The Comanche did not usually eat birds or fish.

Comanche women prepared animal hides for use as tepee covers, clothing, and blankets. Women put up the tepees and

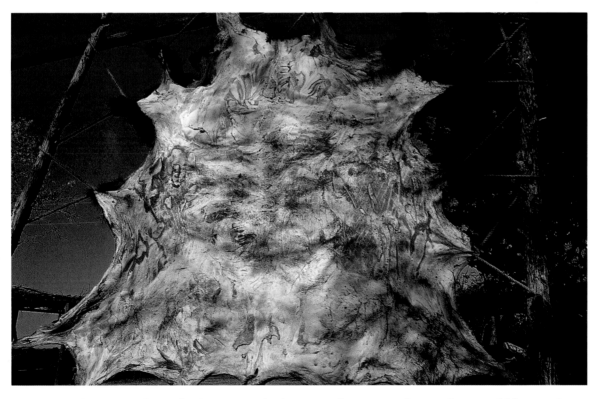

Animal hides were cleaned, then stretched out on frames to dry so they could be used as clothing, blankets, or tepee covers.

The Bone Game

Although the Comanche were often busy around the camp, children and adults liked to play sports and games. From horse racing to arrow-shooting contests to wrestling, the Comanche enjoyed many leisure activities.

One popular game was called the bone game. It was also known as the hands or, after contact with the Europeans, the bullet or button game. Players were divided into two teams. Each team lined up facing the other or formed half circles. While the players sang or beat a rhythm on a drum, players on one team passed a small bone, bullet, button, or other object from team member to team member. Players on the passing team would make many gestures to try to distract the opposing team. When the song ended or the rhythm stopped, the opponents had to guess which player was holding the object. If the opponents guessed correctly, they scored a point and it was their turn to pass the object. If they guessed incorrectly, the team with the object scored a point and continued passing the object. The game was won when one team had scored a certain number of points.

The Comanche played many games, including horse racing, in their spare time.

took them down. They gathered and prepared food for their families. Women and girls picked wild fruits, seeds, nuts, and berries. They also dried meat to make **pemmican**, a favorite food of the Comanche and other native peoples. Women sewed clothing and moccasins from animal hides for their families.

Comanche children were deeply loved by their parents and were rarely punished when they misbehaved. But children were sometimes purposely frightened into behaving properly. Old people might wear costumes to scare

Traditional Comanche clothing included leggings such as these.

them, or the children were told stories about Big Cannibal Owl, who ate bad children.

Children learned by watching and listening to their parents and other adults in the band. Girls followed their mothers around the camp and learned to cook and make clothing. Boys learned from their fathers, warriors, and other male band members. Boys were taught to ride horses even before they learned to walk. By age four or five, boys were skillful riders. (Girls also became expert riders, but

These drawings show examples of clothing worn by the Comanche.

Travois

The Comanche used a travois (tra-VWAH) to carry loads. A travois was made of two long poles with shorter poles placed across. The travois was usually pulled by a horse. You can make a small travois to fit a toy horse.

You will need:

- Several sheets of newspaper to work on
- Two twigs, each about 12 inches long
- Three more sticks or twigs of different lengths: the first one about 9 inches long, the second about 7 inches long, and the third about 5 inches long
- Glue
- String

1. Spread out the newspaper to cover and protect your work area.

2. Place the two 12-inch-long twigs side by side. Place them at an angle so that the tips of the twigs are closer together than the bottoms. (Arrange them as if you are making an "A" without closing the top of the letter.) The tips should be about 2 inches apart. This is the frame for your travois.

3. Glue the ends of the longest of the three remaining twigs to the widest part of the frame.

4. Glue the ends of the second-longest twig across the middle of the frame.

5. Glue the ends of the shortest twig across the top of the frame.

6. Cut a length of string to loop around the neck of your toy horse. Keeping the loop in the string, tie each end of the string around the ends of the travois frame. Slip the loop around your horse's neck. Your toy horse is ready to carry a load.

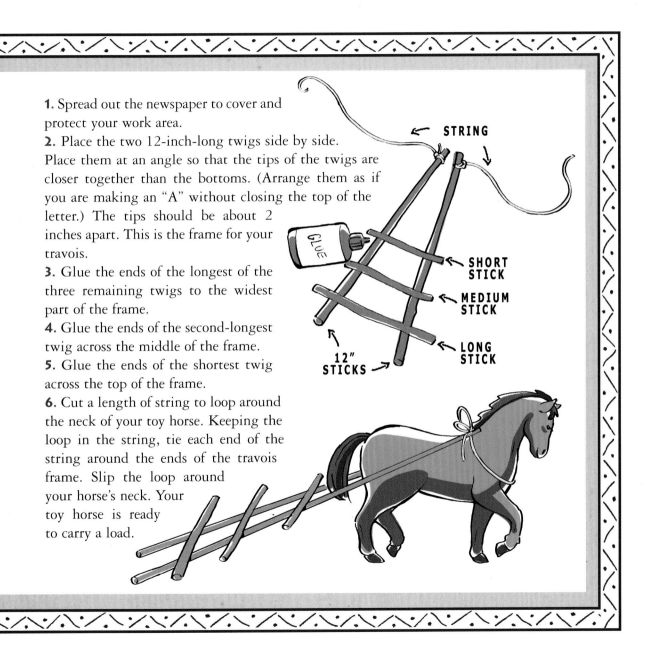

STRING

SHORT STICK

MEDIUM STICK

LONG STICK

12" STICKS →

GLUE

Buffalo Stew

Ask an adult to help you make the following recipe. Wash your hands with soap and water before you begin and after touching raw meat.

- 2 pounds buffalo meat, cut into 1-inch cubes
- 4 quarts water
- 2 pounds red or white potatoes (not russets), cut into bite-sized pieces
- 2 medium carrots, sliced into 1/2-inch pieces
- 1 20-ounce can stewed tomatoes
- 2 celery stalks, cut into 1-inch pieces
- 1 cup barley
- salt and pepper

In a stew pot, brown the buffalo cubes over high heat until seared, about 3 minutes. Add water, potatoes, and carrots, and boil until the vegetables are tender. Add stewed tomatoes, celery, and barley, and boil an additional 5 minutes. Remove from stove and place in a 10-by-12-inch baking dish. Bake at 425 degrees for 20–30 minutes. Season with salt and pepper.

they were not taught as early in life as boys.) By age five or six, boys were given small bows and arrows. Grandfathers usually taught the boys to hunt on horseback.

Comanche clothing was made from buffalo, deer, and elk hides. Women wore dresses, skirts, leggings, and moccasins. Men wore **breechcloths**, leggings, and moccasins. After the arrival of European traders, men wore leather shirts. Children wore smaller versions of the adults' clothing. In cold weather, the Comanche wore knee-high boots and thick buffalo robes.

Men parted their long hair down the middle and often painted their scalps red or yellow. They wore a braid on each side of their head. When going to war or on a raid, they painted their faces red, black, yellow, green, or blue. Women usually wore their hair short, with a part down the middle. They painted their scalps but did not braid their hair. They painted their faces, too, with red and yellow lines. Their ears were painted red, and they put red or orange shapes, usually circles or triangles, on their cheeks.

3 · COMANCHE BELIEFS

The Comanche did not practice an organized religion. They believed that religion was a personal matter between each person and the spirits. The Comanche believed in one main god, the Great Spirit, who created the universe. The sun was a powerful spirit, and the Earth was called "Mother." Some Comanche believed in the Evil Spirit, who brought disaster and unhappiness.

The Comanche also believed that spirits lived in the land, including hills and bluffs, and in water, such as springs and rivers. The Comanche believed in evil little men about 1 foot (0.3 m) tall. The little men carried shields and bows and arrows, and killed people.

Animals were important in Comanche beliefs, because spirits could live within any creature—except horses and

The Comanche believed that powerful spirits lived in buffalo.

dogs—or object. Powerful spirits were said to live in buffalo and could talk to the Comanche. Coyotes could tell when good or bad events were going to happen. Eagles had great power, and their feathers were worn in warriors' hair or placed in headdresses or on shields. Bear and skunk spirits had the power to heal. Guardian spirits lived within elk. Deer contained spirits that had the power over good and evil.

The Comanche prayed to the Great Spirit in private instead of in groups. They were one of the only Plains Indian tribes that didn't perform the Sun Dance, which is performed every spring to renew the land. (The Comanche performed it only once, in 1873.) By the mid-1800s, however, some bands adopted group rituals such as the Beaver Ceremony and the Eagle Dance. The Beaver Ceremony was held to cure illness. The Eagle Dance was performed to provide power for a boy who was becoming a man.

In the 1890s, the Beaver Ceremony and the Eagle Dance were replaced by the peyote religion, introduced by Quanah

Parker. Comanche who felt trapped by the boundaries of the reservation enjoyed the chance to gather together to sing, pray, and take peyote. Peyote is a drug that comes from a cactus plant. The drug caused visions that the Comanche claimed helped them feel free. By 1920, the peyote religion was replaced by the Native American Church, which blended traditional beliefs and Christianity. Today some Comanche still belong to this church, while most have joined other branches of Christianity.

The birth of a child was a joyous event for the Comanche, but the birth of a boy was an especially happy occasion, because he would grow up to be a warrior. The father sometimes named his male children, but he usually asked a **medicine man** or another respected band member to do so. Mothers named female children. The names were given to the children at public naming ceremonies. As children grew up, they were given various nicknames.

At around the age of twelve, a boy went on his first buffalo hunt. If he made a successful kill, he was honored with a feast. After that, he was allowed to go to war. At about age fifteen or sixteen, a young man went on a **vision quest**, a rite of passage during which he would journey away from camp alone to seek spiritual guidance and direction.

As girls grew up, they learned to gather berries, nuts, and roots. They collected water and wood. At about age twelve, girls learned to cook meals, sew clothing, and make tepees.

A medicine man (left) often took responsibility for naming male children in the Comanche tribe.

When a young man liked a young woman, he offered a gift (usually one or two horses) to the young woman's father. Usually, the young man's uncle or another male relative made the offer for him. If the gift was accepted, the man and woman were promised to each other.

The Comanche did not exchange vows in a wedding ceremony. The man simply brought the woman to his tepee. Sometimes, the band held a wedding feast and dance to celebrate the union. One man might have two or more wives at the same time, as Quanah Parker did.

Immediately after a person died, the knees were folded toward the chest and the head was tilted forward. The body was tied in this position and then washed. The face was painted red. The body was dressed in the person's finest clothing. Family and friends gathered, and the body was wrapped in a blanket and taken by horse to the burial place. The dead were placed in a sitting position in a cave or crevice among rocks. Some Comanche placed the dead on log platforms high in the trees.

How the Comanche Came to Be

The Great Spirit gathered swirls of dust from the four directions—north, south, east, and west—and used them to create the Comanche people. These newly created people were strong and mighty. At the same time that the Comanche were formed, a demon was also created. This demon started to bother the Comanche. Hoping to help the people he had created, the Great Spirit threw the demon into a bottomless pit. Wanting revenge, the demon hid in the fangs and stingers of poisonous animals, where it can still harm people whenever it gets a chance to strike.

The Comanche passed down the stories of their creation through each generation.

When a warrior died, female relatives dressed in rags and blackened their faces. They slashed their arms and legs with knives. The warrior's family gave away or destroyed his belongings.

The soul of a dead Comanche, which was believed to live in a person's breath, then traveled to the afterworld. There, the soul joined the souls of friends and relatives.

4 · A CHANGING WORLD

The Comanche reservation was broken up by the U.S. government in 1901 so that individual Comanche families could receive 160-acre (65-hectare) plots of land. Over time, white settlers bought land on the former reservation as well. As a result, the Comanche now live in well-populated areas alongside non-Indians.

Today, members of the Comanche Nation still practice many of their traditional ways. They maintain their language, beliefs, and unique identity as Native Americans. At the same time, they live in the modern world. Many Comanche practice the traditional band structure: various bands have settled together in specific sections of Oklahoma.

The Comanche Nation Tribal Headquarters is located near Lawton, Oklahoma, in the southwestern part of the state.

Modern-day Comanche continue to embrace their traditions.

Tribal leaders are elected by the Comanche. As a tribal community, they are developing services and creating economic and educational opportunities. They operate three casinos, a tourism center, and a recreational water park, which they share with the Kiowa and Apache.

Since the 1890s, when Comanche volunteered to become

This is one of the casinos operated by the Comanche in Oklahoma.

U.S. Army scouts at the site of their reservation at Fort Sill, Oklahoma, Comanche have been actively involved in the U.S. military. During World War II (1939–1945; the United States entered the war in 1941), the Comanche, along with the Navajo, communicated by radio in their own language, which served as a kind of code that the enemy could not break. They were known as Code Talkers. Modern Comanche military societies include the Comanche Indian Veterans Association and the Comanche War Dance Society. The land on which Fort Sill stands covers 95,000 acres (38,000 ha). It contains forty-eight historic sites, including the grave of Quanah Parker.

Today's Comanche are educated at public and private elementary and secondary schools. In Lawton, they pursue higher education at colleges and universities, including Comanche Nation College, Cameron University, and the Great Plains Technical Center. Some Comanche work as ranchers or farmers. Some work as traditional artists, making and selling

LaDonna Harris

LaDonna Harris (1931–) was born in Temple, Oklahoma, and spoke only Comanche until about age five. Harris is known throughout the country as a powerful speaker on behalf of Native Americans. In 1970, she founded Americans for Indian Opportunity, a multitribal organization devoted to developing economic opportunities for Native Americans in the United States. In 1980, she ran for vice president of the United States with the Citizen's Party. Today, Harris is head of an ambassador program she designed for Native Americans from around the country. Young people chosen as ambassadors are sent to other nations to observe the native people and introduce them to traditional Native American ways.

LaDonna Harris is a very influential member of the modern Comanche tribe.

clothing or crafts. Still others make their living as business-people, doctors, lawyers, teachers, police officers, or firefighters.

In the twentieth century, the Comanche, like other native peoples, began to hold several **powwows**, such as the Comanche Nation Fair, every year. The Comanche Homecoming is held each year in mid-July in Walters, Oklahoma. These gatherings offer the Comanche a chance to touch the past as they embrace the future.

Each year, Comanche people gather for powwows such as the Comanche Nation Fair.

· TIME LINE

Before 1700	About 1700	Early 1700s	1830	1835	1840	1844
The Shoshone live in the mountains of present-day Wyoming and Montana.	The Shoshone split into two groups.	The group that would become the Comanche travels into present-day New Mexico.	The U.S. government passes the Indian Removal Act.	The government helps the Comanche make peace with neighboring tribes.	The Council House Massacre leads to a series of attacks between the Comanche and settlers.	Texas and the Comanche sign a peace treaty, but both sides repeatedly break it.

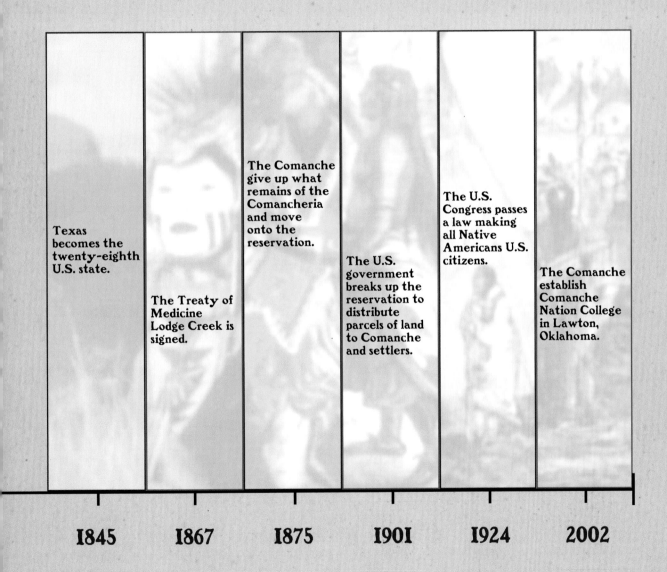

Texas becomes the twenty-eighth U.S. state.

The Treaty of Medicine Lodge Creek is signed.

The Comanche give up what remains of the Comancheria and move onto the reservation.

The U.S. government breaks up the reservation to distribute parcels of land to Comanche and settlers.

The U.S. Congress passes a law making all Native Americans U.S. citizens.

The Comanche establish Comanche Nation College in Lawton, Oklahoma.

1845   1867   1875   1901   1924   2002

· GLOSSARY

band: Group of family members.

breechcloths: Simple garments worn by men that reach from the waist to the upper thigh.

medicine man: A Native American healer and religious leader.

panhandle: The narrow area of land that projects from the northern part of Texas.

pemmican: Dried meat (usually buffalo) that was mixed with fat and dried berries and pounded flat. It could be stored for use during the winter months, so it was important for the tribe's survival.

powwow: A Native American social gathering that includes traditional dances.

raids: Sudden, surprise attacks that are over quickly.

vision quest: Rite of passage in which a Native American youth journeys away from camp to seek spiritual guidance and direction.

· FIND OUT MORE

Books

Bial, Raymond. *The Comanche*. New York: Benchmark Books, 2000.

Egan, Tracie. *Cynthia Ann Parker: Comanche Captive*. New York: Rosen Publishing Group, 2003.

Yacowitz, Caryn. *The Comanche Indians*. Chicago: Heinemann Library, 2003.

Zemlicka, Shannon. *Quanah Parker*. Minneapolis: Lerner Publishing Group, 2004.

Web Sites

www.comanchenation.com
This is the official site of the Comanche Indian Nation. Here you'll find more information about the Comanche.

www.museumgreatplains.org
This site provides more information on the history and culture of the Comanche and other tribes of the Great Plains.

www.nmai.si.edu
The National Museum of the American Indian opened in September 2004 as the newest addition to the Smithsonian Institution. Here you can view the museum's exhibits of Native American art, crafts, and more.

www.redriverhistorian.com/fortsill.html
This is the site of Fort Sill. Here you'll find photos and information about this last remaining active military post that was built during the conflicts between the Indians and the U.S. government.

· INDEX

Page numbers in **boldface** are illustrations.

ABOUT THE AUTHOR

Sarah De Capua is the author of many books, including biographies, geographies, and historical titles. She has always been fascinated by the earliest inhabitants of North America. In this series, she has also written *The Cherokee, The Cheyenne,* and *The Iroquois.* Born and raised in Connecticut, she now resides in Colorado.